Living on the Edge
SURFING

Shane McFee

PowerKiDS press
New York

Published in 2008 by The Rosen Publishing Group, Inc.
29 East 21st Street, New York, NY 10010

Copyright © 2008 by The Rosen Publishing Group, Inc.

All rights reserved. No part of this book may be reproduced in any form without permission in writing from the publisher, except by a reviewer.

First Edition

Editor: Joanne Randolph
Book Design: Kate Laczynski
Photo Researcher: Jessica Gerweck

Photo Credits: Cover, p. 1 © Bill Losh/Taxi/Getty Images, Inc.; pp. 4, 12, 16, 18, 20 © Getty Images, Inc.; p. 6 © North Wind/North Wind Picture Archive; p. 8 © www.istockphoto.com/Tim McCaig; p. 10 © www.istockphoto.com/Seb Chandler; p. 14 © www.istockphoto.com/Ian McDonnell.

Library of Congress Cataloging-in-Publication Data

McFee, Shane.
  Surfing / Shane McFee. — 1st ed.
    p. cm. — (Living on the edge)
  Includes index.
  ISBN: 978-1-4358-3837-6
  1. Surfing. I. Title.
  GV839.5.M39 2008
  797.3'2—dc22

2007037771

Manufactured in the United States of America

CONTENTS

Catch That Wave 5
Captain Cook 7
It's All About the Board 9
What Surfers Need 11
Follow the Waves 13
Surfing Moves 15
Meet Laird Hamilton 17
Danger! 19
Safe Surfing 21
Surf's Up! 22
Glossary 23
Index 24
Web Sites 24

Catch That Wave

Have you ever seen **surfers** at the beach? Maybe you even tried surfing yourself.

Surfing is hard to do. To become really good at this sport takes years of practice. A surfer rides a long, smooth board called a surfboard. He or she lies on the board and paddles out into the ocean. Then the surfer waits for a wave. When a good wave comes, the surfer starts paddling to stay ahead of the wave. He or she must stand up on the board at the right moment to ride the wave.

Does surfing sound fun? Let's find out more!

This man surfs in the waters off of Arica, Chile. The waters off Arica are known for huge, powerful waves.

Captain Cook

Surfing was likely invented in Hawaii in **ancient** times. Hawaiian surfers used much longer boards than the boards we use today. Surfing was a very important part of ancient Hawaiian **culture**. In fact, chiefs had to be good surfers.

Outsiders first learned about surfing in 1778, after the British **explorer** Captain James Cook arrived in Hawaii with his ships. In the end, angry Hawaiians killed Captain Cook when he tried to kidnap their chief. One of Cook's men, named Lieutenant James King, finished Cook's journals, though. He wrote about the Hawaiian surfers and shared this sport with the outside world.

These Hawaiians are surfing near Honolulu, Hawaii, in the 1870s. Today, people come from all over the world to surf Hawaii's waves.

It's All About the Board

Surfboards have come a long way since the heavy pieces of wood used by the ancient Hawaiians. In the 1940s, people began to build surfboards from a much lighter wood called balsa (BAHL-suh). Today, making surfboards is a million-dollar business. Surfboards are lighter and easier to use than ever before. Most surfboards are now made from a special material called polyurethane (pahl-ee-YER-eh-thayn).

Most surfers ride either longboards or shortboards. Longboards are good for beginners. It is easier to catch waves on them. Shortboards are hard to ride, but they can make faster turns.

Most surfboards have fins to help them cut through the water. These look like the fins on a fish.

What Surfers Need

What do you need to surf? You need a surfboard and some waves, of course. There are a few other useful supplies, too.

Surfers who surf in cold water need a special outfit called a wet suit. Wet suits keep the rider from getting too cold in the water. Sometimes surfers will wear wet suits even if the water is warm.

Surfboard wax is very important, too. Surfers use surfboard wax to help their feet stick to the wet board.

Surfers tie the surfboard to their leg with a leash. This keeps the surfboard from drifting away if the rider falls off.

Follow the Waves

Many people like to surf so much they will go anywhere to find the best waves. Some of the best beaches are in Australia, New Zealand, California, and Hawaii.

Surfing has become an important part of American culture. You have likely seen a movie or heard a song about surfing. Surfing is well liked not only in America, though. There is even an **international** surfing **contest** called World Championship Tour Surfing. Men and women **compete** to become the best surfers in the world. Some people are good enough to win **sponsorships**.

These surfers compete in the 2007 Monster Energy Pipeline Pro off the north shore of Oahu, Hawaii.

Surfing Moves

Catching waves is only the first step to surfing. Good surfers can do special moves on their boards. Surfers must also be able to turn their surfboards in order to stay ahead of the wave. Surfers call this carving.

As a wave moves toward the shore, its top starts to curl over. Sometimes a surfer will ride inside this curl. This is called **tube** riding because it looks like the surfer is inside a tube. Other times a surfer will ride the board with all 10 toes hanging over the front of the board. This move is called hanging 10.

This surfer is riding the tube of a wave he caught in Mexico. Riding the tube is also called getting barrelled.

Meet Laird Hamilton

One of the best surfers in the world is an American named Laird Hamilton. Hamilton is also a model. He was born in San Francisco and grew up in Hawaii. Hamilton has been a surfer for most of his life.

Hamilton does not like to compete in surfing competitions because he thinks surfing is an art and not a contest. He has done many **dangerous** surfing tricks and has surfed some of the biggest waves in the world. He is married to the famous model and volleyball player Gabrielle Reece.

Laird Hamilton has always pushed surfing to its limits. He learned to surf when he was between the ages of two and three!

Danger!

Surfing is fun, but it can also be dangerous. Drowning is the biggest danger to surfers. Waves carry the boards at very high speeds. If surfers fall while surfing, they may hit their head on the board. Surfers can also hit underwater objects, like rocks. If a surfer is knocked out while surfing, he or she might drown.

Sometimes sharks or other sea animals may try to take a bite out of surfers. Smart surfers always keep their eyes open. They know what kinds of dangerous sea animals live in the waters where they surf.

A surfer falls from his board here. A fall can be scary, but it is important to stay calm and find your way back to the top of the water.

Safe Surfing

Does surfing sound too dangerous? Careful surfers do not have much to worry about.

Surfers should always watch the weather report on television before heading to the beach. This can tell them what kinds of waves they will see. If the water is not safe for swimming, it is unsafe to surf, too.

Surfers should not surf alone. Most surfers surf with another surfer or in groups. This lets surfers look out for each other. If a surfer is in trouble, the rest of the group can come to his or her aid.

These surfers know it is safer to surf in a group. It is also important to surf waves that match your skill.

Surf's Up!

Does surfing sound like fun? If you live near the ocean, you can take surfing lessons. You can take lessons if your family vacations at a beach, too. In the United States, surfing is well liked in California, Hawaii, North Carolina, and other states on the coast.

You can ask your mother and father to help you find a surfing teacher. Keep in mind that it can take years to become a good surfer. Plan to spend a long time practicing.

Surfing is a great way to enjoy the outdoors. Maybe it is the sport for you.

GLOSSARY

ancient (AYN-shent) Very old, from a long time ago.

compete (kum-PEET) To go against another in a game or test.

contest (KAHN-test) A game in which two or more people try to win.

culture (KUL-chur) The beliefs, practices, and arts of a group of people.

dangerous (DAYN-jeh-rus) Might cause hurt.

explorer (ek-SPLOR-er) Someone who travels and looks for new land.

international (in-tur-NA-shuh-nul) Having to do with more than one country.

sponsorships (SPON-ser-ships) People or companies that pay for and plan something.

surfers (SERF-erz) People who use boards to ride ocean waves.

tube (TOOB) Something that is long and has a small opening, like a straw.

INDEX

A
Australia, 13

C
California, 13, 22

H
Hawaii, 7, 13, 17, 22

K
King, James, 7

L
longboard(s), 9

N
New Zealand, 13

S
shortboard(s), 9
surfboard wax, 11

W
wet suit(s), 11
World Championship Tour Surfing, 13

WEB SITES

Due to the changing nature of Internet links, PowerKids Press has developed an online list of Web sites related to the subject of this book. This site is updated regularly. Please use this link to access the list:
www.powerkidslinks.com/edge/surf/

www.ingramcontent.com/pod-product-compliance
Lightning Source LLC
Chambersburg PA
CBHW041121070526
44584CB00002B/239